THE STORY OF THE
OKLAHOMA CITY THUNDER

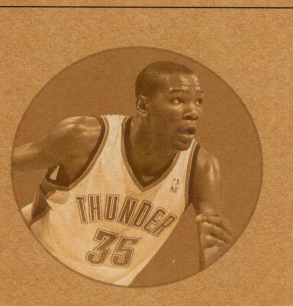

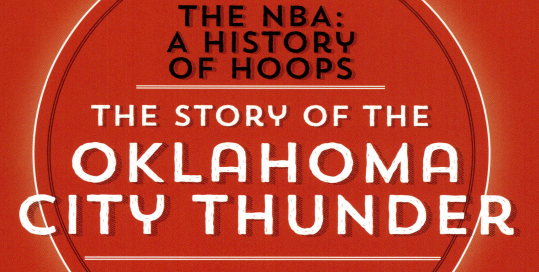

THE NBA: A HISTORY OF HOOPS

THE STORY OF THE OKLAHOMA CITY THUNDER

NATE LeBOUTILLIER

CREATIVE EDUCATION

Published by Creative Education
P.O. Box 227, Mankato, Minnesota 56002
Creative Education is an imprint of The Creative Company
www.thecreativecompany.us

Design and production by Blue Design
Art direction by Rita Marshall
Printed in the United States of America

Photographs by Corbis (CHRIS KEANE/Reuters, Reuters, Chris Szagola/ZUMA Press), Getty Images (Tim Defrisco, James Drake/Sports Illustrated, Ron Hoskins/NBAE, Walter Iooss Jr./NBAE, George Long/Sports Illustrated, George Long/WireImage, Melissa Majchrzak/NBAE, Fernando Medina/NBAE, Layne Murdoch/NBAE, Joe Murphy/NBAE, NBA Photo Library/NBAE, NBA Photos/NBAE, Dick Raphael/NBAE, William R. Sallaz/NBAE, Larry W. Smith/NBAE, Rick Stewart, Terrence Vaccor/NBAE, Rocky Widner/NBAE, Jeremy Woodhouse)

Library of Congress Cataloging-in-Publication Data
LeBoutillier, Nate.
The story of the Oklahoma City Thunder / Nate LeBoutillier.
p. cm. — (The NBA: a history of hoops)
Includes index.
Summary: An informative narration of the Oklahoma City Thunder professional basketball team's history from its 1967 founding as the Seattle SuperSonics to today, spotlighting memorable players and events.
ISBN 978-1-60818-442-2
1. Oklahoma City Thunder (Basketball team)—History—Juvenile literature. I. Title.

GV885.52.O37L43 2014
796.323'6409766'38—dc23   2013039310

CCSS: RI.5.1, 2, 3, 8; RH.6-8.4, 5, 7

First Edition
9 8 7 6 5 4 3 2 1

Cover: Forward Kevin Durant
Page 2: Guard Thabo Sefolosha and forward Kevin Durant
Pages 4-5: Forward Kevin Durant
Page 6: Guard Russell Westbrook

TABLE OF CONTENTS

COURTSIDE STORIES

INTRODUCING…

LOOKING FOR A LEADER

OKLAHOMA CITY IS HOME TO CORPORATIONS, COLLEGES, PARKS—AND PRO SPORTS TEAMS.

The Oklahoma Land Rush of 1889 was one of the strangest chapters of pioneering in United States history. On the 22nd of April, under pristine blue skies, boomers and prospectors lined up—if they hadn't already been hiding out and making their claim unscrupulously—at high noon and raced by horse and foot to claim some 2 million acres of land in an all-out burst for settlement.

The rush into the "Unassigned Lands" meant that many cities in what would someday become the state of Oklahoma were literally built in a day. Included in this list were the towns of Stillwater, Norman, Guthrie, and Oklahoma City. Guthrie and Oklahoma City gained populations of some 10,000 pioneering folk in a single day, most of whom camped out temporarily in "tent cities." While Guthrie was the front-runner to become Oklahoma's

capital, it never grew and eventually ceded the status to Oklahoma City, which now features a metropolitan area home to more than one million residents.

Another group rushed into town when a National Basketball Association (NBA) franchise formerly known as the Seattle SuperSonics came to Oklahoma City in 2008. Native Oklahoman Clay Bennett had purchased the team from Seattle businessman Howard Schultz, the chief executive officer (CEO) of Starbucks Coffee, in 2006. Bennett had bought the team on the condition that he would make a sincere effort to keep the team in the state of Washington's largest city, Seattle. But just two years later, the NBA approved the move, and Oklahoma was the franchise's destination.

Before the move to Oklahoma, though, the franchise was born into the NBA in 1967 in Seattle and spent four decades in the great city of the Pacific Northwest. Seattle is home to the Boeing Company, which builds some of the world's largest jets, and thus the team was named the SuperSonics in the powerful aircraft's honor. The Sonics' colors of green, white, and gold were implemented, and, seemingly as fast as the speed of sound, the new hoops team hit the hardwood.

HAYWOOD'S HARDSHIP

From 1971 to 1975, SuperSonics fans were treated to the high-energy game of forward Spencer Haywood. After growing up poor in Mississippi, Haywood resolved to make a better way for his family, and in 1969—as a 20-year-old who had played just 2 years of college ball—he signed with the American Basketball Association's (ABA) Denver Nuggets, since the NBA didn't allow underclassmen in its draft. Following a long battle in court, Haywood won a legal appeal to enter the NBA and came to Seattle in 1970. This led to the NBA's "hardship rule," which allowed early draft entrance to players who could prove financial hardship. Seattle fans loved Haywood's rim-rocking style, but on the road, Haywood took some verbal abuse from those who thought he didn't yet belong in the league. "I was *in* the court one day and *on* the court the next day, and they were booing and throwing bottles at me," he later recalled. Kevin Garnett, the 2004 NBA Most Valuable Player (MVP) and a former "hardship" case himself, thanked Haywood in his MVP acceptance speech, saying, "I'm forever grateful to [him] for leading the way."

LENNY WILKENS

As a sophomore and junior, Lenny Wilkens never even went out for his high school basketball team. He didn't think he was good enough. Luckily for Wilkens— and the rest of the basketball world—a friend convinced the young guard to try out his senior year. The smooth-shooting and slick-passing Wilkens proved a wizard on the high-school court, inspiring team play in much the same way he later would in the NBA. He joined the St. Louis Hawks via the 1960 NBA Draft and led his team to the Finals as a rookie, and then was traded to the Sonics in their second season of existence in 1968–69 and averaged 22.4 points per game. His next three seasons in Seattle, Wilkens served as player/coach, and the team improved each year. But the Sonics traded him away, and it would be five seasons before the team welcomed him back as head coach only. In 1979, the SuperSonics, under Wilkens's guidance, won their only NBA title. "I loved that team," Wilkens said. "We believed in ourselves and knew we would find a way to win no matter what. That was special."

The SuperSonics' inaugural season went down in the record books with 23 wins and 59 losses. Though guard Walt Hazzard provided plenty of offense, the Sonics seemed to lack leadership. Seattle solved that problem after the season by trading Hazzard to the Atlanta Hawks for veteran guard Lenny Wilkens, who served double-duty as both player and coach.

Another early Sonics star was Spencer Haywood, an explosive young forward known for his amazing leaping ability and rare shooting touch. "When Spencer was on, he could demoralize the other team single-handedly," explained Sonics center Bob Rule. "He'd pull up from 25 feet and launch one [shot] after another into the rafters. Somehow the ball would usually come down *snap* in the center of the basket."

Other popular players included guard "Downtown" Freddie Brown, known for his long-range bombs, and Don "Slick" Watts, a slim but smooth point guard characterized by his uncanny speed, quick hands, and the bright green headband he wore around his bald head. After arriving in 1973, Watts won over Seattle fans with his hustle and community involvement.

"In the 10 years of the Sonics, I don't know of one player on a par with Slick Watts as far as desire on the court and ability to make people happy," team owner Sam Schulman once said. "I wish I had 12 Slick Wattses on my team."

It wasn't until 1977, however, that the Sonics built a true winner. Watts was traded away for feisty point guard Dennis Johnson, and acrobatic guard Gus Williams joined him in the backcourt. Inside, forwards Paul Silas and John Johnson and centers Marvin "The Human Eraser" Webster and rookie Jack Sikma did the dirty work. Wilkens—who had left the franchise in 1972 and retired as a player in 1975—returned in a more comfortable, coach-only role, and the Sonics made the NBA Finals, only to fall short against the Washington Bullets in seven games.

Although dispirited, the Sonics vowed that they would be back, and they spent the 1978–79 season fulfilling that vow. Manning the forward positions were Lonnie Shelton—the team's enforcer—and John Johnson, while Sikma controlled the pivot. Williams and Dennis Johnson continued to form a magnificent guard duo, and Brown and Silas provided great bench support. Together, these players formed the "Seattle Seven." After a 52–30 season, Seattle tore through the playoffs to face the Bullets again in the NBA Finals.

FRED BROWN

POSITION GUARD
HEIGHT 6-FOOT-3
SUPERSONICS SEASONS
1971–84

When the NBA painted a three-point arc on its courts for the first time in 1979, long-range basketball shooters everywhere rejoiced, not least among them "Downtown" Freddie Brown. Brown, who had a successful, high-scoring collegiate career at the University of Iowa, was drafted by both the SuperSonics and the ABA's Kentucky Colonels. But he chose the Sonics and became that rare player who spends a long career (13 seasons, in Brown's case) with the same team. Brown, with his trademark goatee and Afro, came off the bench as a sixth man for much of his pro career, and by 1978–79, the year the Sonics won the only championship in franchise history, Brown was considered such an integral part of the squad that he was named team captain. The 14 points per game he averaged that season didn't hurt, either. Upon retirement from the NBA, Brown went into banking but remained in Seattle. "The city still cherishes our championship," Brown said. "When I'm out and about, I hear the constant chatter of, 'Get back in the game, Fred.'"

SONIC REIGN

REBOUND LEADER JACK SIKMA (#43) ROUNDED OUT THE CHAMPIONSHIP SONICS TEAM.

After losing to the Bullets 99–97 in Game 1 in Washington, D.C., Seattle proved unstoppable for the rest of the Finals. The Sonics destroyed the Bullets four games to one, bringing Seattle its first NBA championship. Williams averaged nearly 30 points per game in the series, and Dennis Johnson, who was all over the floor for Seattle, won the Finals Most Valuable Player (MVP) award. "Last year we didn't know what to expect in this series, but we came in with our eyes open this time," said Johnson. "We did everything we had to do to win."

The victory was particularly sweet for Wilkens, who—before he would retire from coaching—would become the NBA's all-time leader in coaching victories yet win just the one championship, with Seattle. "I still remember when I took over that team," Wilkens later recalled with a laugh. "I

SLICK'S STYLE

Fashion trends come and go in the NBA. Short shorts, long shorts. Afros, cornrows. Tattoos, "air" shoes. One trend has come, gone, and come back again: the headband. Don "Slick" Watts, who played point guard for the SuperSonics for five seasons in the mid-1970s, was one of the first to make headband-wearing fashionable, sporting it cockeyed on his hairless crown. "All these guys wearing headbands now are just following Slick Watts," said John Lucas, a former NBA guard and coach. "But he was more than a guy with a headband. He was a good point guard who really knew how to distribute the ball." Watts's best season was 1975–76, when he averaged 13 points, a league-leading 8.1 assists, and 3.2 steals per game. Although he was traded away to the New Orleans Jazz and missed the Sonics' championship season of 1978–79, Watts returned to the Pacific Northwest and taught physical education in Seattle's schools following his NBA career. "It's good to see the kids come back with the headbands," Watts said. "It lets people know that Slick Watts is still alive."

19

had heard general managers and other people say it was the worst team ever. And when I turned them around, all of a sudden everyone said, 'Well, we all knew they had the talent.'"

The next season, Seattle fans watched their club achieve its best record yet, 56–26, with the core of its championship team intact. But a new Western Conference foe, the Los Angeles Lakers, had risen to power behind center Kareem Abdul-Jabbar and precocious rookie point guard Magic Johnson. The Lakers whipped the Sonics in the 1980 Western Conference finals, four games to one.

The SuperSonics' 1980–81 season was a disaster. The veteran Silas retired, the high-scoring Williams got into a contract dispute that led him to sit out the entire season, and the rough-and-tumble Shelton was routinely shelved by injuries. To top it off, the Sonics had traded Dennis Johnson, the hero of their lone championship, before the season to the Phoenix Suns for aging guard Paul Westphal. Although Johnson was moody, he was only 25 years old, with his best seasons still ahead of him.

The trade did not pan out well for the Sonics. Although Westphal averaged a respectable 16.7 points a night, he played in just 36 games as the Sonics went 34–48 and missed the playoffs, while Johnson led a successful Suns outfit in scoring and steals. Williams rejoined the team in 1981–82, and the Sonics made it to the second round of the Western Conference playoffs before losing out. The rest of the early '80s were marginally successful in Seattle.

In 1985, the Sonics made Lenny Wilkens a team executive and hired Bernie Bickerstaff as coach. Seattle soon featured a new, exciting collection of players, too. Forward Tom Chambers impressed fans with his scoring and spectacular dunks, guard Nate McMillan emerged as the team's defensive stopper, guard Dale Ellis gave the Sonics lethal three-point shooting, and 6-foot-9 forward Derrick McKey added versatility.

Another new Seattle star was Xavier McDaniel. The fourth overall pick of the 1985 NBA Draft and a fan favorite, "The X-Man" was a skilled rebounder and scorer at the forward position, and a head-shaven intimidator in the paint. "People always say [Chicago Bulls guard] Michael Jordan started the look, and I just laugh," said McDaniel of his trendsetting style choices. "Actually, I started the bald head. Slick Watts was the first guy in the NBA to do it, but he was long retired when I arrived. It became my trademark, and then it became everyone's trademark, and I almost had to grow an Afro back."

Although the Sonics' 1985–86 season was a losing endeavor that ended 31–51, it was notable for featuring one of the strangest postponements in sports history. On January 5, 1986, the Suns were in town to play the Sonics at the Seattle Center Coliseum, but in the second quarter, with the Suns ahead 35–24, a crack in the roof let in a Seattle tradition: rain. Puddles formed on the court, and the game had to be rescheduled for the next day. The Suns went on to win the NBA's only rain delay, 114-97.

In 1986–87, the Sonics posted a 39–43 record during the regular season but sneaked into the playoffs as the seventh seed. Seattle shocked its first-round opponent, the Dallas Mavericks, three games to one, then upended the Houston Rockets in the second round, four games to two. "Bernie had us believing that if we walked in fire, we would come out fine, with no scratches,"

NATE McMILLAN

POSITION GUARD, COACH
HEIGHT 6-FOOT-5
SUPERSONICS SEASONS
AS PLAYER 1986–98
AS COACH 2000–05

As a heady backup guard, Nate McMillan won over many Sonics fans with his intelligent play and rugged defense. Affectionately known as "Mr. Sonic," McMillan played out all 13 of his NBA seasons in Seattle and then began coaching the team immediately after his playing career ended. For two years, he learned the coaching ropes as a Sonics assistant, and by the beginning of the 2000–01 season, he was head coach. The Sonics made the playoffs twice in McMillan's five-year tenure as head coach, but when it came time to lock him up with a new contract in 2005, the Seattle front office balked, and McMillan slipped away to coach for the Portland Trail Blazers, just to the south, on Interstate 5. "This was the time for me to move on," said McMillan. "I needed a different challenge, a different opportunity." Many fans called McMillan's move the beginning of the end for basketball in Seattle, and they may have been right. Bob Weiss was hired as McMillan's replacement in 2005–06 but was fired just 30 games into the job. The Sonics left Seattle for Oklahoma City in 2008.

PAUL SILAS

THAT '70S RERUN

The Sonics made the NBA Finals three times in their history, and twice their championship opponent was the Washington Bullets. In back-to-back years, 1978 and 1979, the green-and-gold Sonics, with their strong backcourt, met the red-white-and-blue Bullets, with their strong frontcourt. Fittingly, each team garnered one championship trophy out of the deal. The first go-round, the series was an epic battle that spanned seven games. The Sonics lost 1978's Game 7 more than the Bullets won it as Seattle's guards shot horribly, leaving Seattle fans with a bitter taste in their mouths. "That first year, we were just overmatched," said Sonics coach Lenny Wilkens. "Washington was big, strong, and smart, and they wore us down. The next year, however, we learned how to play them and had the type of team that could better deal with the things they did." Sure enough, the second time was a charm for Seattle, as it lost Game 1 but won the next four straight to claim victory. Said Bullets guard Bernie Bickerstaff, "They were just better than we were the second time. They were hungry, and they played like it."

said McDaniel. Although the Lakers swept the Sonics in the Western Conference finals, high-level basketball seemed to be back in Seattle.

In 1988, Seattle added muscular power forward Michael Cage to its lineup and promptly posted its first winning record in four years. Even though two mediocre seasons followed, two more rising stars emerged: highflying forward Shawn Kemp and multitalented point guard Gary Payton. Kemp had jumped directly from high school to the NBA, joining the Sonics in 1989 at the age of 19. With his long arms and explosive vertical leap, "The Reign Man"—a pun on Seattle's rainy weather—thrilled local fans with an array of rim-rattling slams.

Payton, meanwhile, quickly earned a reputation around the league for two things: tenacious defense and trash-talking. He was quick, but he was also incredibly strong for his size. Nicknamed "The Glove" because he covered his man as tightly as a glove fits on a hand, Payton played suffocating defense and burned with intensity. Away from the court, however, Payton showed a softer side by creating his own charity—the Gary Payton Foundation—to help underprivileged children.

XAVIER McDANIEL'S AGGRESSIVE PLAY HELPED HIM AVERAGE 20.7 POINTS PER GAME.

A RUN AT THE BULLS

McDANIEL OFTEN PUT ON A SHOW FOR FANS, SURGING SKYWARD FOR MIGHTY DUNKS.

In 1992, George Karl was hired as Seattle's new head coach, and in 1993–94, the Sonics posted an NBA-best 63–19 record. German forward Detlef Schrempf and sleepy-eyed forward Sam Perkins added veteran intelligence and excellent outside shooting, but it was the talented Payton–Kemp combination that led the way. "They've always been the two young guys," said Coach Karl. "Now they've blossomed into perennial All-Stars."

But postseason success eluded the top-seeded Sonics when they were shocked by an eighth-seeded Denver Nuggets squad and its young center, Dikembe Mutombo, in the opening round of the 1994 playoffs. The defeat was most bitter, as it was the first time in NBA playoffs history that an "eight" had defeated a "one."

In 1995–96, the Sonics rebounded gallantly from their crushing 1994 playoff loss in a newly refurbished KeyArena.

GARY PAYTON

POSITION GUARD
HEIGHT 6-FOOT-4
SUPERSONICS SEASONS
1990–2003

Nicknamed "The Glove" for his ability to seemingly fit right on top of the opponent he was guarding, Gary Payton was the floor general for many successful Sonics teams throughout the 1990s. Tall and wiry for a point guard, Payton's game was hounding his man and getting steals on defense and then either setting up teammates with nifty passes or taking it to the hole himself on offense. He wasn't a bad shooter, either; in 1999–2000, he led the NBA in three-pointers made with 177. As of 2014, Payton was the only point guard in the history of the NBA to win the Defensive Player of the Year award, which he did in 1995–96. "You think of guys with great hands," said Kevin Johnson, a rival point guard who played for the Phoenix Suns. "Gary is like that. But he's also a great individual defender and a great team defender. He has all three components covered. That's very rare." Payton played for four different teams at the end of his career, winning a championship as a backup with the Miami Heat in 2005–06.

"LOOK, WE GOT THIS FAR, AND A LOT OF PEOPLE DIDN'T EXPECT THAT. A LOT OF PEOPLE DIDN'T THINK WE'D BEAT THE BULLS IN ONE GAME."

— HERSEY HAWKINS ON THE 1996 FINALS AGAINST THE BULLS

After powering their way to a franchise-best 64–18 record and the Western Conference championship, they met the 72–10 Chicago Bulls—owners of the greatest single-season record in league history—in the NBA Finals. Although Seattle won two games, star guard Michael "Air" Jordan led Chicago to the championship. "Look, we got this far, and a lot of people didn't expect that," said Seattle guard Hersey Hawkins. "A lot of people didn't think we'd beat the Bulls in one game."

The next few campaigns were mostly disappointing as fine regular seasons dissipated into postseason shortcomings. Former player Nate McMillan took over as Seattle's coach in 2000. McMillan relied on the veteran Payton to guide the Sonics on the court until The Glove was traded to the Milwaukee Bucks for shooting guard Ray Allen in 2003. The 2002–03 Sonics finished 40–42. It was the club's first losing record in 16 years.

But in 2004–05, the Sonics bounced back, exceeding expectations with an impressive work ethic. Behind the play of the high-scoring Allen, explosive forward Rashard Lewis, locally grown point guard Luke Ridnour, and rebounding workhorse Reggie Evans, the Sonics won the Northwest Division with a surprising 50–32 record. In the playoffs, they beat the Sacramento Kings in the opening round before falling to the eventual league champion Spurs.

Unfortunately, this run of success was short-lived. The Sonics fell into a rut for the next three seasons, posting losing records and, worse, losing fan support. The winds of change were beginning to blow in Washington.

FOSTER CITY

When Hurricane Katrina ravaged the city of New Orleans in August 2005, neighboring communities were called on for help, and one of the cities answering the call was Oklahoma City. Due to massive damage, New Orleans Arena would not be able to host the New Orleans Hornets' home games, posing the immediate question, "Where will the Hornets play?" Cities suggested in addition to Oklahoma City included Baton Rouge, Kansas City, Louisville, Nashville, and San Diego. After some deliberation, Hornets owners decided on Oklahoma City, largely because it featured the 19,675-seat Ford Center. The Hornets played 35 of their home games in 2005–06 in Oklahoma City, with the other 6 played in other venues. The arrangement worked out so well for the Hornets that they stayed in Oklahoma City for the 2006–07 season while New Orleans recovered. Following the Hornets' return to New Orleans in 2007, NBA commissioner David Stern deemed Oklahoma City NBA-ready should the league expand or a team want to relocate, announcing, "I can say without reservation that Oklahoma City is now at the top of the list."

29

ON TO OKLAHOMA

KEVIN DURANT'S STELLAR ROOKIE SEASON PROVED THE FRANCHISE WAS IN GOOD HANDS.

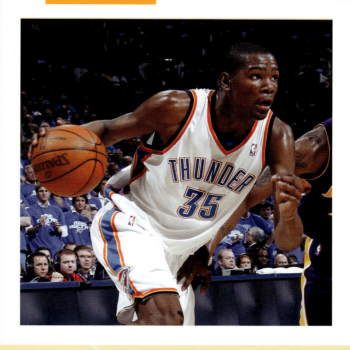

uperSonics fans finally had something to cheer about in 2007. That summer, the team used the second overall pick in the NBA Draft to obtain Kevin Durant, a 6-foot-9 forward. Even though the Sonics sputtered badly overall, Durant averaged 20.3 points per game in 2007–08 and won the NBA's Rookie of the Year award. "It's good to shine some light on our team," said Durant, whose team finished a franchise-worst 20–62. "You know, a lot of people aren't real fond of our team right now."

Clay Bennett's flirtations with relocation turned to reality when, in 2008, Washington lawmakers refused to finance a new arena for the Sonics, who were losing money because attendance at home games had dropped. "It gets down to a fairly simple notion," Bennett said. "A private investment demands a return, and this investment will not

CALLING DOWN THUNDER

When Oklahoma City businessman and Seattle SuperSonics owner Clay Bennett got the okay from the NBA and federal judges to move the team to his hometown in April 2008, the city of Seattle retained rights to the "SuperSonics" name and the team colors of green and gold. That meant that Bennett's team spent some time as "the yet-to-be-named Oklahoma City team." Proposed names included Wind, Barons, Marshalls, Energy, and Bison. Finally, on September 3, 2008, the new name and colors were announced. The team would be called the Thunder, and its new colors would be blue, orange-red, and yellow. "There's just all kinds of good thunder images and thoughts, and the in-game experience of Thunder," Bennett said. "It's very powerful." Players modeled the new uniforms as some 200 fans showed up to a downtown office building where the team was headquartered. "I love 'em," said coach P. J. Carlesimo. "The biggest mistake you can make with uniforms is going crazy with too much detail. We talked about respecting the heritage of the NBA, and I think we did it."

provide a return." In July 2008, it was officially announced that the Sonics were leaving Seattle for Oklahoma City. Subsequently, Oklahoma City sped up its process of preparing to host an NBA team, which the city had done in a temporary capacity in 2005–06 and 2006–07 when the local Ford Center hosted the New Orleans Hornets, who had been displaced by the Hurricane Katrina disaster of 2005.

As the franchise prepared to start a new chapter, a new name was chosen: the Thunder. New uniforms were also designed, and new season tickets were sold as the team began to acclimate to a new home. The Thunder's top pick in the 2008 NBA Draft was guard Russell Westbrook, a talented and versatile playmaker at both ends of the court. Although boisterous, appreciative crowds showed up at the Thunder's

KEVIN DURANT

POSITION FORWARD
HEIGHT 6-FOOT-9
SUPERSONICS / THUNDER
SEASONS 2007–PRESENT

Thunder fans quickly grew fond of lanky, sweet-shooting forward Kevin Durant in his first season in Oklahoma City. It was no wonder, since Durant could score from both inside and out and was a virtual bucket-filling machine. But the beginning of Durant's career as a basketball player occurred far away, in the town of Capitol Heights, Maryland, at the Seat Pleasant Activity Center. Durant would go there early in the morning to hone his game against older, more physical players. He had many coaches early on who pushed him, too, especially Taras Brown, who led the young Durant through workouts, and, often, to a place called Hunt's Hill. When Durant didn't perform as Brown required, he would make the youngster sprint up steep Hunt's Hill and then backpedal down, often as many as 25 times. Sometimes, he'd let Durant rest at the top of the hill, where one could see the domes and beauty of the nation's capital, Washington, D.C. "He wouldn't quit," Brown said of Durant. "I would give Kevin days off, and he'd show up at the rec. He wanted to live in the gym."

home games, Westbrook and his teammates started the 2008–09 season by losing 12 of their first 13 contests.

With the Thunder struggling, head coach P. J. Carlesimo was fired and replaced by interim coach Scott Brooks. "We have to get better no matter who the coach is," said Durant. "To start off like we did my first year, and now this year, is tough to deal with. If we continue to work hard, things will start to turn around for us."

Durant was right. Under Coach Brooks's direction, the team's play improved as young stars Durant, Westbrook, and forward Jeff Green redoubled their efforts and began playing with more cohesion. By late in the season, the Thunder were giving opponents trouble, even if their final 23–59 record didn't necessarily reflect their promising improvement.

SCOTT BROOKS SOON FIGURED HOW TO BEST UTILIZE PLAYERS SUCH AS KEVIN DURANT.

RUMBLE THE BISON PUMPS UP THE HOME CROWD AS THE THUNDER'S OFFICIAL MASCOT.

THE THUNDER RUMBLES

FORWARD SERGE IBAKA'S DEFINITIVE REJECTIONS EARNED HIM THE NICKNAME "IBLOCKA."

Added to the mix of up-and-coming talent in Oklahoma City was shooting guard James Harden, a former star at Arizona State and the team's first-round draft pick in 2009. Harden was considered one of the better all-around players in the Draft, and he gave the Thunder a third star-caliber player behind Durant and Westbrook. "I feel that I can do different things well as far as shoot the ball, create for different teammates, and play defense," said Harden. "Whatever the coach needs me to do, I think I can do pretty well."

Durant continued his ascent as a scoring master and led the NBA with 30.1 points per game in 2009–10, and for the first time since moving to Oklahoma City, the Thunder made the playoffs. There they drew the defending champion Lakers, who downed the Thunder in six hard-

JEFF GREEN AVERAGED 15.1 POINTS AND 6 REBOUNDS PER GAME IN THE 2009–10 SEASON.

fought games. "There's good chemistry, a group of four really good scorers, and they've got some good role players that can assist them," said Lakers coach Phil Jackson. "They're talented, it looks like they work well together. They're without a large center, but they can get the job done."

During the next season, the Thunder addressed their need for a solid big man by trading their third-leading scorer, Green, to the Celtics for no-nonsense center Kendrick Perkins. With Perkins, shot-blocking wonder Serge Ibaka, and steady rebounder and defender Nick Collison manning the paint, the Thunder were ready to roll. After rolling up a 55–27 regular season record, Oklahoma City whipped the Nuggets and survived the Memphis Grizzlies in the playoffs to face the Dallas Mavericks.

The Mavericks were led by phenomenal-shooting big man Dirk Nowitzki, who was enjoying the postseason of his life. Though the Thunder and Mavericks split the first two games, Nowitzki and the Mavs won the next three to take the series. "Their time will come, but it's not now," said Dallas coach Rick Carlisle of the Thunder. "We feel like now is our time to move on." Carlisle was proven correct as the Mavericks eventually went on to take the NBA title with Nowitzki earning Finals MVP honors.

Coming so close to making the Finals drove the Thunder to work even harder, and, after the owners' lockout that threatened to wipe away the 2011–12 NBA season ended, Durant and Company hit the court. In the shortened season, the Thunder charged through the schedule and into the playoffs, beating three titans of recent NBA-championship mettle. First, Oklahoma City swept the defending champion Mavericks

RUSSELL WESTBROOK

POSITION GUARD
HEIGHT 6-FOOT-3
THUNDER SEASONS
2008–PRESENT

When Russell Westbrook first donned an Oklahoma City jersey and joined the ranks of the NBA in 2008, jaws began dropping league-wide. The precocious point guard had spent only a pair of seasons at the college level playing for the University of California, Los Angeles (UCLA), and in that time had only begun to tap his potential. Teamed with second-year star forward Kevin Durant, Westbrook's game rose like so many of his gravity-defying slam dunks. In his rookie season, Westbrook averaged 15.3 points and 5.3 assists per game—more, in either category, than he'd ever averaged at UCLA. By his third season, his points and assists had jumped to 21.9 and 8.2, respectively, easily among the league leaders, as he made his first NBA All-Star team. In 2011–12, Westbrook and Durant led Oklahoma City to the NBA Finals. "How can you not love this guy?" said Thunder coach Scott Brooks after the Thunder signed Westbrook to a five-year contract extension in 2012. "The guy plays with so much passion, he plays with toughness, he plays for the team, and he's improved every month since we've had him."

PRIZED DEFENDER NICK COLLISON POSTED IMPRESSIVE OFFENSIVE STATISTICS AS WELL.

COURTSIDE STORIES

A GOLDEN TRIO

As members of the U.S. men's basketball team at the 2012 Summer Olympics, Oklahoma City Thunder teammates Kevin Durant, Russell Westbrook, and James Harden (pictured) avoided a long off-season of sitting around and lamenting their recent 2012 NBA Finals defeat at the hands of the Miami Heat. Roughly a week after the Finals, the three joined the rest of the players chosen to represent Team USA as they prepared for the Olympics, which were to be held in London, England. The coaching staff soon learned of the Thunder players' great work ethic. "Westbrook was the first one into practice, going a thousand miles an hour," said assistant coach Mike D'Antoni. "Durant doesn't want to come out of any scrimmages. Harden was the same way. These are special kids." Once in London, the trio impressed a global audience by helping the U.S. to an undefeated record and the gold medal. "It was just an honor and a blessing to be on this team, to represent your country in the Olympics," said Durant, who led the U.S. team in scoring. "And to be able to do it with Russ and James made it even better."

to exact revenge for the previous season. The second round, it took the Thunder just five games to eliminate the Lakers (champions in 2000, 2001, 2002, 2009, and 2010), and then, in the Western Conference finals, the San Antonio Spurs (champions in 1999, 2003, 2005, and 2007).

n the NBA Finals, the Thunder matched up against the Miami Heat and the triple threat of star players LeBron James, Dwyane Wade, and Chris Bosh. Oklahoma City started the series with a 105–94 win in front of an adoring home crowd, with Durant scoring 36 points and Westbrook scoring 27 to lead the way. But then James caught fire, leading the Heat to a close victory in Game 2 and then helping Miami to three more consecutive wins to close out the title en route to being named Finals MVP. "They're going to be a team to be reckoned with for a lot of years,... and they're going to use this experience as motivation," said James of the Thunder. "You know this is not the last time we'll see Oklahoma City."

The next off-season, Oklahoma City shocked its fans when it sent Harden and three other players to the Houston Rockets in exchange for high-scoring guard Kevin Martin, young prospect Jeremy Lamb, and future draft picks. Durant and Westbrook carried the extra burden as the team finished 60–22, an improvement on its previous regular season's winning percentage. The stage seemed set for another Thunder-ous run at the NBA Finals.

In the opening round of the playoffs, Harden lit up his former teammates for 20 and then 36 points in the series' first two games, yet the Thunder won both. Westbrook was not so lucky. After colliding with a Houston player in

Game 2, he injured his knee and was out for the remainder of the playoffs.

The Thunder regrouped enough to finish off the Rockets in six games, but the loss of Westbrook was too much to overcome in their second-round matchup with the Memphis Grizzlies, who upended the Thunder in five closely contested matches. "It's tough to swallow right now," said Durant after his team's early playoff exit, "but I'm sure we're going to look back on this down the line and appreciate this tough time."

The Thunder began the 2013–14 season with their eyes trained on the championship trophy, starting 19–4. Though Westbrook wasn't yet back to full playing time, Durant shouldered the bulk of the scoring load, recording at least 25 points for 39 consecutive games. With young players such as seven-foot center Steven Adams and forward Andre Roberson stepping up, the Thunder prepared for the battle ahead in the playoffs.

Westbrook returned to form as Oklahoma City fought off the Grizzlies in round one, but the Spurs bested the Thunder in the Western Conference finals. Although Durant, Westbrook, and the rest of their teammates were disappointed, Coach Brooks countered, "Kevin and Russell, they should be proud. They've led us to places that we want to get to, and I'm proud of what they've done. I'm proud of who they are, and I'm sure our fans feel the same way."

The Thunder have much to be proud of in recent seasons in Oklahoma City, and the franchise's history during the Seattle years gleams bright as well. But talented superstars such as Kevin Durant and Russell Westbrook attract more than local fans. Fans of basketball across the U.S. and even around the world are excited to see what kinds of wonders the Thunder will call down next.

INDEX